A Gift For

_____

_____

From

_____

_____

Date

_____

A Girl's Diary of Prayers

by
Mary Hollingsworth

Illustrated by
Lois Rosio Sprague

OLIVER
NELSON

A *division of*
THOMAS NELSON PUBLISHERS
Nashville

Text copyright © 1992 by Mary Hollingsworth, 3950 Fossil Creek Boulevard, Suite 203, Fort Worth, Texas 76137

Illustrations copyright © 1992 by Lois Rosio Sprague, 217 West Avenue, Wayne, Pennsylvania 19087

Copyright © 1992 by Educational Publishing Concepts, Inc., Wheaton, Illinois

Scripture quotations are from the NEW KING JAMES VERSION of the Bible. Copyright ©1979, 1980, 1982, Thomas Nelson, Inc., Publishers.

Library of Congress Cataloging–in–Publication Data
Hollingsworth, Mary, 1947–
        A girl's diary of prayers / by Mary Hollingsworth ; illustrated by
    Lois Rosio Sprague
            p. cm.
        Summary: A collection of prayers for special times in a girl's
    life, including prayers from the Bible, prayers to sing, and prayers for important days.
        ISBN 0-8407-9169-0
        1. Girls—Prayer-books and devotions—English. [1. Prayers.
    2. Prayer books and devotions.] I. Sprague, Lois Rosio, ill.
    II. Title.
    BV283.G5H57 1992
    242'.833—dc20   92-3096
                                                                                    CIP
                                                                                    AC

Printed in the United States of America.
1 2 3 4 5 6 7 — 97 96 95 94 93 92

❀ ❀ ❀ ❀ ❀ ❀ ❀ Contents ❀ ❀ ❀ ❀ ❀ ❀ ❀

How You Can Use This Book 7

All About Prayer 11

- What Is Prayer? 11
- When Should I Pray? 13
- What Should I Say When I Pray? 15
- How Do I Know God Hears My Prayers? 18
- Will God Always Answer My Prayers? 23
- Where Should I Pray? 24
- How Should I Pray? 26

Special Prayers for Special Times 29

- Prayers for Happy Times 30
- Prayers for Sad Times 34
- Prayers for School 40
- Prayers for Home 44
- Prayers for Church 49

- Prayers When I'm Afraid 51
- Prayers When I'm Worried 54
- Prayers of Praise 57
- Prayers of Thanks 60
- Prayers When I'm Sick 63
- Prayers Before I Sleep 64
- Prayers Before I Eat 67

Prayers in the Bible 71

Prayers to Sing 79

Famous Prayers 87

Prayers for Important Days 99

People I Want to Pray For 107

My Prayer Diary 121

My Personal Prayers 133

How You Can Use This Book

Some things are private, right? There are just some things you can't tell anybody else–not even your best friend. But you really need to talk to somebody. So what can you do?

Here's some great news! You can talk to God. He'll listen to everything you need to tell Him. And He won't tell anyone else–ever.

You can tell Him about things that make you happy or sad. You can tell Him about things that make you afraid or worried. You can talk to Him about problems at school, at home, or with your friends. You can laugh when you talk to Him, or you can cry. He won't mind because He loves you so much.

Talking to God is called prayer. And prayer is what this book is all about. We made it small so you can take it with you wherever you go.

7

You can take it to school and read it during study hall or before a test. You can take it in the car on trips; it will break up the highway boredom. You can take it on picnics to read in a quiet place by yourself. You can even take it to bed at night to help you fall asleep.

This book is private. It's yours and nobody else's. You'll find pages to write on toward the back. You'll find prayers you can sing somewhere in the middle. And you'll find a prayer diary where you can keep up with answers to your prayers.

You're going to like this book a lot. It's your own personal diary of prayers. So if your name isn't there already, start by putting your name in the front. Then check out the different parts of the book you can use. God's waiting to hear from you.

—Mary Hollingsworth

A Girl's Diary
of Prayers

All About Prayer

What Is Prayer?

Pretend that you're in your bedroom all alone. The door is closed so nobody can hear you. You're in your favorite jeans and shirt. And you're lying on your bed munching some chips and sipping a soda. Something exciting has just happened, and you can't wait to tell somebody. So you pick up the phone and call your best friend in the whole world.

While you're telling your friend the good news, you laugh and talk happily. She's excited for you too. You can tell by her laugh and her voice. She's happy because you're happy. When you hang up, you feel great. It's fun to share your secrets with someone you can trust... someone who loves you...someone who is happy for you.

That's what prayer is like. It's telling secrets to your best friend in the whole universe–God. You can tell Him anything, and He won't laugh at you or make you feel silly. Your feelings are important to God because He loves you. He will be happy when you're happy and sad when you're sad. He will help you to solve problems or to make plans for the future.

He'll help you at school, at home, or at church.

Yes, God is always there to answer your prayer calls. And His line is never busy! Just say, "Dear God, I need to talk to You," and He'll be listening to every word.

When Should I Pray?

The Bible says we should "pray without ceasing." But how could you do that? You'd never get anything else done, would you?

Let's look at it this way. When can you talk to your best friend? Just about anytime, right? You're walking down the street together and you think of something you want to say.

So you just say it. You're in the school cafeteria and have something to say. You just say it, don't you? Or maybe you think of something to say while you're playing outdoors. Just yell it out! You don't have to have a special time to talk to your best friend, do you? Since she's always around, you can talk to her anytime.

Well, you don't have to have a special time to talk to God either. Just say what you're thinking anytime. After all, God is always right there beside you. And He's your friend. So you can talk to Him any old time. That's what "pray without ceasing" means: talk to God anytime and all the time. He'll love it.

What Should I Say When I Pray?

One time Jesus' friends said to Him, "Lord, teach us to pray." In other words, they were asking, "Jesus, what should we say when we pray?"

So Jesus gave them a sample prayer to help them. He said,

"Our Father in heaven,
Hallowed be Your
  name.
Your kingdom come.
Your will be done
On earth as it is in heaven.

Give us this day our
   daily bread.
And forgive us our
   debts,
as we forgive our
   debtors.
And do not lead us into
   temptation,
But deliver us from the
   evil one."

—*Matthew 6:9-13*

Did Jesus mean that His
followers had to pray these
exact words? No. He was
just showing them the kinds
of things they might want to
pray to God about. You can
pray for food. You can pray
for Him to help you do right
things. But you can also pray
for God to forgive you for
wrong things you do and to
help you forgive other
people who do wrong to you
(everybody does wrong
things once in a while). And
you can pray for Him to help
you beat the devil.

The truth is, you can say anything you want to God. Of course, you should talk to Him with respect and honor—after all, He is God! And you should always tell Him the truth about things. You might as well; He already knows the truth anyway. You can't fool God, you know.

How Do I Know God Hears My Prayers?

Since God doesn't talk aloud to you, how can you know that He hears you when you pray? Here are some ways to know.

It's in His Book. God speaks to you and answers your prayers through the Bible. So, when you pray to God for help, listen to Him talk to you about that problem by reading His Book.

If you pray for Him to give you a new friend, read what the Bible says about friendship and love. When you learn to be a good friend, you're sure to find a new friend. Then you'll know God answered your prayer by helping you find the friend you asked for.

You get what you asked for. The easiest way to tell is getting what you prayed for. Maybe you pray to God to help you get along better with your mom and dad. Pretty soon you find yourself working harder to be helpful and kind to your parents, and things get better. You got what you asked for, and so you know God heard your prayer.

A friend or family member gives you the answer. Sometimes God uses other people to give you the answer to your prayer. You might ask God to help you decide whether to sing in the church chorus or to be in the puppet ministry at church. And before long the chorus director asks you to sing a solo. Then you know that God has said, "I'd like you to sing in the chorus." He gave you the answer through a friend.

Things just don't work out.
You pray that God will help
you get elected class
president at school, but one
of the other girls in your
class wins the election. That
doesn't mean that God didn't
hear your prayer or care
what you want. It means He
thinks it's better for you not
to be president right now.
His answer this time is no.
Because He cares about you,
God can't always say yes.

God says, "Wait." There
are times when you ask for
something that God knows
(because He's wiser than
you) you're not quite ready
for yet. So God doesn't say
yes, and He doesn't say no.
He is just silent. You may
think He didn't hear your
prayer, but really He's just
saying, "Wait a little while."

Then one day, when you don't expect it, you'll get it. That's what happened to Abraham in the Bible. He prayed and prayed for a son, but God didn't send him one. Then, when Abraham was one hundred years old, his son, Isaac was born. God had been saying, "Wait."

22

Will God Always Answer My Prayers?

Yes. As we've been learning, He may say yes or no or wait. But He always hears you, and He always answers–one way or another. What you have to do is learn how to listen to Him. You listen by reading His Book. You listen by hearing Him speak to you through your friends or family. And you listen by watching what happens in your life. If you listen carefully, you'll hear Him answer your prayers one by one.

A good way to keep up with the answers to your prayers is to use the part of this book near the back called "My Prayer Diary." You can write down what you prayed and how God answered your prayer.

Where Should I Pray?

You can pray anywhere! That's the best part of all. You don't have to be in a church building to talk to God. That's because He's everywhere. He's in the park, at school, in your home, in the mall, at the movies, at birthday parties, and at youth retreats. Anywhere you go, God is there with you–just like your best friend.

In the Bible there are people who prayed on mountaintops, in gardens, on rooftops, in the temple, in synagogues (church buildings), and in caves and deserts and rivers. Some prayed in kings' palaces and out under trees. They prayed everywhere!

You can pray to
Him walking down a
country road or
standing on top of a
huge building
downtown. You can
talk to Him in your
room at home or
standing in line at
the amusement park.
Don't worry; He'll
hear you and answer
every time because
He loves you so much.

How Should I Pray?

When you read in the Bible about prayer, you find people praying in all kinds of ways. Some people stood up and lifted their faces toward the sky. Some people got down on their knees. Others lay stretched out face down on the ground. Still others lay in their beds.

God doesn't say exactly what position you have to be in to talk to Him. You can pray any way you want to pray.

Think about it. The whole idea is this: You can talk to God anywhere anytime about anything. You can talk to Him everywhere every day. You can talk to Him inside or outside, aloud or silently, standing or sitting or kneeling, laughing or crying, thanking Him or asking Him for things. God's your best friend in the whole world, and He wants to hear everything you have to say. He loves you and wants to share every part of your life. So why not talk to Him now?

28

Special Prayers for Special Times

Special times in your life require special prayers, don't they? But sometimes it's hard to think of what to say to God at those special times. Here are some prayers to get you started talking to God at those really special times in your life. Once you get started, it will be easy for you to just say what you need to say yourself.

Feeling Good

Dear Father, I'm so
happy today. The
weather's great, school
was fun, and I feel
good. Thanks for
happy days like today,
Lord! In Jesus' name.
Amen.

Good Grades

Dear Lord, it's a great day! I think I made a good grade on my test at school today, and that makes me happy. Thanks for helping me remember what I had studied. I love You, God. Amen.

Saturday–No School

Dear God, today is Saturday, and I love it. It's fun to have time to do what I want to do. Maybe You and I can just spend some time together today. Thanks for Saturdays, Lord. Amen.

Summertime

Good morning, Lord. Thanks for summer and happy times with my friends and family. It's nice not having to go to school every day. I like lying in the cool grass under a shade tree and reading books just for fun. Help me to remember to read Your Book often too. I love You, Father.

Thanks for just always being there for me to talk to. In Your Son's name I pray. Amen.

Vacation

O Father in heaven, we're leaving on vacation today, and I'm so excited. Thanks for letting us be together and have this chance to enjoy each other. I know we're going to see some wonderful things in Your world. And I guess You can tell that I'm happy today. Please be with us and keep us safe as we travel. And please help me to be patient and kind to the others while we're gone. You're the greatest, Lord! Amen.

Sunshine

Dear God, I'm so glad the sun is shining. It's a beautiful day, and I can't wait to get outside. Your sunshine makes me feel warm inside and outside. It makes the grass look greener and the flowers look brighter and more colorful. Thanks for the sunshine, Lord. You're so kind and good to me every day. I love You for taking such good care of me and my family. And thank You for Your Son. Amen.

Friend Is Moving Away

Dear Father, I'm so sad today. My best friend is moving away. I don't know when I'll ever get to see her again. She's so important to me, God. I'll really miss her. Please help me to be brave when she goes. You'll still be there for me, won't You? I'll need You now more than ever. In Jesus' name. Amen.

I'm Moving Away

Dear God, why do we have to move away? It makes me so sad to leave all my friends at school and at church. And I'm scared to have to go to a new school and church where we're moving. I don't know whether those new kids will like me or not. And I don't know whether my new teachers will be nice or not. Father, help me to know that You'll take care of me no matter where I go. Help me to be brave and even excited about getting to meet new people. I love all my old friends, Lord. Please help me to love the new friends You're going to give me. I love You, God. In Your Son's name. Amen.

Death of a Pet

O Lord, please help me. I just found out that my pet died today, and my heart hurts so bad. I don't understand very much about death. I hope it didn't hurt when my friend died. I know You'll take good care of this little creature that You made. I'd really appreciate Your giving some special attention to my little friend. Thanks for listening, God. Amen.

Parents Divorcing

Dear God in heaven, I really need to talk to You today. My parents are getting a divorce. I guess You already knew that. What will I do now? Our family won't be together anymore. And that makes me so sad. Will You please help me to be strong through this thing? I can't do this alone. Help me to be brave for my parents too. Please help me to understand why this is happening. And help me to know that it's not my fault. Most of all, please just be there when I need to talk to You, okay? Amen.

Death of Mother

Dear Father, help me. I'm so mixed up and sad. I don't understand why my mama had to die. She was so special, and I don't know what I'm going to do without her. Who's going to take care of me? And who's going to teach me things I need to know? Please, Lord, help me to understand why this has happened. Help me to know that You won't leave me too. I need to know that You're there all the time. God, please show me how to help my dad too. We'll need each other more than ever now. Help me, God, and please take care of my mom. I know she's with You now. In Jesus' name. Amen.

Death of Father

O God, why can't I stop crying? My daddy's gone to live with You, and I'm happy for him. But I miss him so much, and it hurts so badly. I can tell that Mom is hurting, too, because she cries a lot. Father, I guess You'll be my only daddy now. I'm sure glad that You're still there for Mom and me. Please help us to understand why my dad had to die. Show us what You want us to do now. I want to be brave for my mom, but I feel so sad and weak. Please make me strong. Help us to know that everything will be okay as long as we depend on You. I love You, Father. Amen.

Prayers for School

Before a Test

Dear Lord, I have an important test today. I've studied hard, and I've learned as much as I can. Could You please help me to remember what I've studied and learned today as I take this test? With my hard work and Your help, I know I can do just fine. Please be with me today. And thanks. In Jesus' name. Amen.

When I'm Tempted

Father, another kid offered me some drugs at school today. I said no, but it was hard. A lot of the kids really give me a hard time for not trying drugs. And it's not easy to keep saying no, even though that's what I want to do. Please help me to keep saying no, Lord. Make me strong when I face temptation. Help me to remember that Jesus said no when the devil tempted Him. I want to do right, God. Please help me. Amen.

When I Fail

O God, I really messed up this time, and I'm so embarrassed. I didn't do it on purpose, but I feel like such a failure. Please help me to know that everyone messes up once in a while. And help me to do better next time. Father, please let me understand that You love me even when I fail. And I love You too. In Jesus' name. Amen.

When I Win

Dear Lord, I'm so
happy! I won today!
It feels so good to
be a winner once
in a while. Please
help me to be the
right kind of winner.
Don't let me tease or
make fun of anyone
who lost. Remind me
that I lose sometimes
too. Just please help
me to be a humble but
happy winner and to
enjoy this special blessing
from You. Thank You for
making me a winner today,
Lord. Amen.

42

When I Compete

Dear God, I want You to be proud of me. We're having a contest at school, and I want to win so much. Several of my friends are entering the contest too. That means that some of us have to lose. Please help me to be fair, Lord, as I compete with the other kids. If I win, help me to be kind about it; and if I lose, help me to be nice about it. Whatever happens, help me to act like Your child. In the name of Christ. Amen.

Talking About Others

O Lord, help me not to talk about other kids in school in a mean way. Teach me not to repeat lies and stories I hear about other students. I don't want to hurt other people, and I know that words can hurt more than anything else. Give me the courage to walk away when my friends start telling stories about other kids. Help me to act as Jesus would act. I pray in His name. Amen.

Prayers for Home

At Mealtime

Dear Father, thank You for the wonderful food that You give us every day. And thanks for my mom and dad who fix it for me. Help me to use the energy this food gives me to do my best for You. And please help me to remember to share my food and blessings with others. In Jesus' name. Amen.

At Bedtime

Good night, Lord. I'm really tired tonight and ready for some rest. Thank You for sleep. Please let the rest I get tonight be enough to see me through the things I need to do for You tomorrow. I pray that You will protect me while I sleep. I love You, Father. Amen.

Trouble with Mom

Dear God, thank You for my mom. She's a really great mom, and I know that she loves me so much. I'm sorry that I sometimes hurt her feelings. We just don't seem to understand each other very well. Please help me to be kinder and more polite to Mom. I really love her, and I want so much for us to get along. I don't want to make her sad. In Jesus' name. Amen.

Trouble with Dad

Dear Lord, why can't I get along better with my dad? He's so important to me, but he doesn't ever seem to have much time for me. I need to be with him more because I love him so much. Sometimes it seems that he treats me like a baby. I know he doesn't mean to; he's just trying to take care of me. Help him to understand that I'm growing up. And help me to remember that he just doesn't want to see me get hurt. Help me to be sweeter to him, and help him to be the kind of father that You are. Amen.

Trouble with Brother/Sister

Dear Father, I'm upset and need to talk to You about it. I'm always getting into arguments with my brother /sister. I don't know why because I really like him/ her. We're just different, I guess. We don't like the same things, and we don't do things alike. Please help us to know that it's okay for us to be different and that neither one of us is right or wrong. Help us to learn to look harder for things we can agree on. Please help us not to argue and fight, Lord. In Your Son's name. Amen.

47

Thanks for My Family

Good morning, Lord. I
just wanted to say thanks
for my family. My mom
and dad are really neat
people, and I love them a
lot. Thanks for letting
me be born to such
great parents. And
thanks for my
brother(s)/sister(s),
too. We have a lot of fun
together most of the time.
I really love them, too,
even though I don't tell
them very often. It's a great
family, God! Thanks for giving
them all to me. Amen.

Prayers for Church

For My Teacher

It's Sunday, Father, and I'm going to Sunday school. Thanks for my teacher at church. He/she really makes our Bible lessons fun and interesting. I know it must take him/her a lot of time to get ready to teach us every week. Please help me to tell him/her thanks. I love You, Lord. In Jesus' name. Amen.

For My Minister

Dear God, thank You for my minister. He's so kind and happy. I really like him a lot. Please bless him and his family, Lord. They work really hard for You, and I know it is not always easy. I'd like to help them somehow if I can. Will You please show me what I can do? Thanks. Amen.

For the Church

Dear Lord, thank You for
Your church. There's so
much love here, and it
feels so good to be with
other people who love
You. Thanks for giving us
the church where we can
help each other. I know
it really cost You a lot of
pain to send Jesus to
save us. Thank You for
loving us that much.
Help me always to live
the way You want me to
live. And please help me
to tell other people about
Jesus. In His name. Amen.

50

Prayers When I'm Afraid

Of the Dark

Dear Father, I'm scared. I sure hope You're there listening to me right now. I don't know why I'm afraid of the dark, but I am. Maybe it's because I can't see what's around me. Please make my heart not feel afraid, Lord. Help me to remember that You're the Lord of the darkness, too, and that You're always with me–night or day. Help me to sleep now knowing You'll take care of me. In Jesus' name. Amen.

Of a Storm

Dear God, I'm afraid of this storm. Please help me not to be so scared. The thunder makes so much noise that I can't sleep very well. And the wind makes scary sounds–it sounds so powerful! Father, help me to remember that You control the wind and the thunder. Make me know that You are the One who tells the storms which way to go. Keep me safe from Your storm, Lord, and help me to be brave. Amen.

Of Being Alone

O Lord, I really hate being alone. I get really scared sometimes when I'm by myself. Please help me to remember that You're always with me, no matter where I am. And help me to know that You're here with me right now; I'm not really alone at all. Keep me safe, Father, and help me not to feel afraid. Stay with me, Lord; I need You. In Jesus' name. Amen.

Of a Stranger

Dear Father, help me. There's a stranger here, and I'm scared. I don't really know what to do. Please help me remember what I've been taught to do about strangers. Please lead me to safety, Lord. I'm depending on You. In Jesus' name. Amen.

Of Trying New Things

Dear God, please help me to be brave. I've never done this before, and I'm afraid I might fail. I'm afraid my parents or friends will be disappointed in me. I really want to do it, so please just give me the courage to do my best. Then, Lord, would You please just take my best and help it along a little bit? Thanks. With Your help I know I can do it. I love You. Amen.

Prayers When I'm Worried

About My Schoolwork

Dear Father in heaven, I'm worried about my schoolwork. I don't seem to be doing very well right now. I'm not sure why. Maybe I haven't really been trying as hard as I can. Please help me not to worry about it so much but to get busy and work a little harder. Then maybe I won't have anything to worry about. In Jesus' name. Amen.

About My Parents

O Lord, I'm so worried about my mom and dad. They don't seem to be getting along very well right now. I hear them arguing and fighting sometimes. I'm afraid they might get a divorce, and I don't want that. Please help them to love each other more, Lord. And help me not to worry so much about them. I know that You can take care of this problem. And...could You please hurry? Thanks. Amen.

About a Friend

Dear God, my friend's in trouble. She's/he's been acting really funny lately. I'm afraid she/he may be taking drugs or doing something harmful. I know it doesn't really help for me to worry, Lord, so could You please show me some way to help my friend? Help me to say something or do something that will help her/him right now. And then help me to believe that You'll take care of the rest. I love You, Lord. In the name of Jesus. Amen.

About a Pet

Dear Father, I'm so worried about my pet. He's/she's so sick right now, and I'm afraid he/she might die. I love him/her so much, God, and I don't want to lose him/her. Will You please take care of my little friend? And please help me not to worry so much but to trust in You instead. In Jesus' name. Amen.

About Someone Who's Sick

My Lord and God, You know that _____ is really sick right now. And I'm so worried. I don't know what to do to help, and I'm afraid of losing her/him. Father, please make her/him well–You're the only One who can do it. And help me to know that You will take care of her/him in the way that's best. I won't worry so much, Lord, knowing that You're on the job. And thanks. Amen.

Prayers of Praise

About God's World

My dear Father and friend, I know You made the whole world and everything that's in it. Your world is so beautiful, God! Thank You for letting me live here and enjoy it. No one else could ever make anything as wonderful as You have. I love You and praise Your name with all my heart. In Jesus' name. Amen.

About Jesus

O God of heaven, thank You so much for Jesus. I know that it must have hurt You terribly to let Him die for us. I can't even understand why You would do it for me. I don't deserve it. But I'm so thankful that You loved me enough to allow Jesus to come to earth and save me. You're the greatest, God! And I love You so much. In His name. Amen.

About the Holy Spirit

Dear Lord, I really don't understand very much about Your Holy Spirit, but I want to know Him better. You're so much greater than I am; Your Son is so wonderful; and Your Spirit is so powerful. How can I ever praise You enough for the beautiful things You do for me every day? My heart is so thankful it feels as if it will burst. Praise the name of Jesus. Amen.

About God's Power

Dear Father, I know that You're the most powerful being in the universe. There's no other person or thing that can match Your strength. I bow down before You, Lord, because I respect You so much. And I praise Your powerful and mighty name above anything else in my life. You are the Lord Most Powerful. And I love You. Amen.

Prayers of Thanks

For My Family

Thank You, God, for my family. They're so important to me, and I love them so much. Thank You for my mom and dad, for my grandparents, for my brothers and sisters, and for my aunts and uncles and cousins. Thanks for everyone in my family, Lord. In Jesus' name I pray. Amen.

For Life

Dear Lord, thank You for making me and giving me life. I really love living on Your earth. I love the people I know and the places I go. And I love Your Son Jesus who died in my place on the cross so I can live with You someday in heaven. Thanks for life, Lord. It's great! In Jesus' name. Amen.

For Food, Clothes, and Home

O Father, You've been so good to me. You have given me plenty of good food to eat, nice clothes to wear, and a warm house to live in with my family. Help me to be happy with the wonderful things You've given me. And thank You for taking such good care of me, Lord. I love You so much. Amen.

For Friends

Dear God in heaven, thank You for my friends. They make life so much nicer. We have so much fun laughing and singing and playing together. I know that You especially chose these friends for me to have. And I'm so thankful to You. In the name of Christ I thank You. Amen.

At Home

Dear Lord, I'm not feeling very well today. I have a fever, and my throat's sore. I had to stay home from school. Could You please help me to get well, Lord? I can't do it by myself, but I know that You can do it. Please help me. In Jesus' name. Amen.

Prayers When I'm Sick

In the Hospital

Dear Father, I really hate this hospital. I have to stay in this bed, and there's just not much to do that's fun. Besides, I feel really bad, and my parents are worried about me. Father, could You please help me to get better soon so I can go home? You're the only One who can make me well. And, God, could You please hurry? Thanks. Amen.

For a Long Time

Dear God, I've been sick for a long time now, and You know how tired I am. My body feels bad all the time, and I can't seem to get better. Could You please make me well, Father? My parents and the doctors don't seem to be able to do too much. You're the only One I can turn to, God, and I know that You can heal me. I'll be waiting to hear from You, Lord. Please make it soon. In the name of Jesus. Amen.

After a Good Day

Good night, Father. It's been a good day today. Thanks for happy times at school and at home. I pray that You'll protect me now while I sleep. Help me to rest and be ready for another good day tomorrow. I love You, Lord. And thank You for Jesus. Amen.

After a Hard Day

Dear Lord, I'm really tired tonight. Today was a hard day at school. So please help me to go to sleep right away and to rest really well tonight. Please bless my family as they sleep too. And keep us all safe through the night. In Jesus' name I pray. Amen.

For a Busy Tomorrow

Dear Father, tomorrow's going to be a busy day. I'm really excited about it too. I know it's going to be hard for me to sleep tonight, but could You please help me to rest? I'll need to be full of energy tomorrow. So I'd appreciate Your helping me to sleep well and dream happy dreams. Thank You for taking care of me today. In Christ's name. Amen.

For the Whole Family

O Father, please protect me while I sleep. And please bless my mom and dad, my brothers and sisters, and my grandparents. Things have been hard for our family lately, Lord, so would You please help everyone to rest well tonight so that we can get through tomorrow a little better? I love You, Lord. In Jesus' name. Amen.

Prayers Before I Eat

For All the Wonderful Things

Dear God, thank You for all the wonderful things You do for us every day. Thank You now especially for this food and the energy it gives us. Thank You, too, Lord, for the person who prepared this food for us. In Jesus' name. Amen.

For Food and Clothes and Shelter

Dear Lord in heaven, You always take such good care of me. You give me food to eat, nice clothes to wear, and a comfortable place to live. Thank You for all these things. And please help me never to forget how much You love me. And, Father, let me be more like Your Son Jesus by sharing my food with others. In His name I pray. Amen.

For All the Food We Need

Dear God, You're so good to us all the time, and I love You for that. You've given us all the food we need. But sometimes we take our food for granted and just *expect* You to give it to us. Thank You, Father, for our food and for taking such good care of us. In Jesus' name I pray. Amen.

For Different Kinds of Foods

Dear Father, thank You for all the blessings You give us every day, like the food we have on the table in front of us right now. Help me to learn to eat all different kinds of foods and to enjoy them. And, Lord, thanks for the person who fixed this food for us to eat. I love You, and I love him/her. Amen.

Prayers in the Bible

Talking to God in prayer is nothing new. People have been praying to God ever since He created the world.

The Bible is God's Holy Word. We can learn more about prayer by looking in the Bible. Here are some of the prayers that God put in His Word to help us know how to pray too. You might want to pray a prayer like one of these some time.

A Prayer for Guidance

Show me Your ways, O LORD;
Teach me Your paths.
Lead me in Your truth and teach me,
For You are the God of my salvation;
On You I wait all the day.

Remember, O LORD, Your tender mercies and Your
    lovingkindnesses,
For they are from of old.
Do not remember the sins of my youth, nor my
    transgressions;
According to Your mercy remember me,
For Your goodness' sake, O LORD.

—Psalm 25:4-7

A Prayer for Help

Do not withhold Your tender mercies from me, O Lord;
Let Your lovingkindness and Your truth continually
    preserve me.
For innumerable evils have surrounded me;
My iniquities have overtaken me, so that I am not able
    to look up;
They are more than the hairs of my head;
Therefore my heart fails me.

Be pleased, O Lord, to deliver me;
O Lord, make haste to help me!

—Psalm 40:11-13

A Prayer for Protection

Hear my cry, O God;
Attend to my prayer.
From the end of the earth I will cry to You,
When my heart is overwhelmed;
Lead me to the rock that is higher than I.

For You have been a shelter for me,
A strong tower from the enemy.
I will abide in Your tabernacle forever;
I will trust in the shelter of Your wings . . . .

So I will sing praise to
   Your name forever,
That I may daily
   perform my vows.

—*Psalm 61:1-4, 8*

Psalm 23

The Lord is my shepherd;
I shall not want.
He makes me to lie down in green pastures;
He leads me beside the still waters.
He restores my soul;
He leads me in the paths of righteousness
For His name's sake.

Yea, though I walk through the valley of the
        shadow of death,
I will fear no evil;
For You are with me;
Your rod and Your staff, they comfort me.

You prepare a table before
    me in the presence of
    my enemies;
You anoint my head with
    oil;
My cup runs over.
Surely goodness and
    mercy shall follow me
All the days of my life;
And I will dwell in the
    house of the LORD
Forever.

—*Written by* KING DAVID
New King James Version

Prayers to Sing

Do you like to sing? Then these prayers are for you! These are prayers put to music. God loves to hear His children pray and sing. He must especially love to hear them sing a prayer to Him, don't you think? Some of these prayer songs are perfect to share with a friend or your Sunday school class. You can sing them together as you talk to God. You don't have to be a great singer either because God said "make a joyful *shout*" when you sing. He doesn't care whether you have a good voice or not—it's your heart He wants to hear. So tune up and sing a prayer to God.

As Long As I Live

Mary Hollingsworth

Traditional

Dear   God up in Hea-ven,   I bow down   to   worship You,   to

honor You,   my   Sav-ior   and   Lord.   I'll   praise   and   I'll

love You   as   long   as   I   live. Amen.   A - men.   I'll   praise

and I'll love You as long   as   I live. Amen.   A - men.

Father, Keep Me Safe and Happy

Mary Hollingsworth

Traditional

Fa-ther, keep me safe and hap-py through the day and the night.

Fa-ther, help me do the things I know are right _____.

Keep me al - ways in Your sight _____.

81

Teach Me, Lord

(ROUND)*

Mary Hollingsworth

Traditional

Teach me to be Your ser - vant, Lord; Teach me to share Your

Ho - ly Word; Teach me all the Christian joys I've seen and heard.

*HINT: SING THIS ONE AS A ROUND WITH A FRIEND.

Help Me, Father

Mary Hollingsworth

Beethoven

1. Help me, Fa - ther; I'm a - fraid. Give me courage; make me brave.
2. Help me, Fa - ther; I'm a - lone. Make me brave while on my own.
3. Help me, Fa - ther; I'm so sad. Cheer my heart, and make me glad.

Jesus Always Cares

Mary Hollingsworth

Traditional

When I'm lone-ly, sad or wor-ried, Je-sus al-ways, al-ways cares.
When I'm scared or hav-ing trou-ble, Je-sus al-ways, al-ways cares.
When I'm tired or sick or an-gry, Je-sus al-ways, al-ways cares.

He's my friend and my big Bro-ther; so, my fears He al-ways shares.

He's my friend and my big Bro-ther; Je-sus al-ways, al-ways cares.

Prayer Song

Mary Hollingsworth

Traditional

1. Fa - ther hear me as   I   pray.   Keep me safe   with You today.
2. Je - sus is my   clos-est friend. Thank You, God, for send-ing Him.

Help me be both kind   and good. Help me do the things I should.
Let   me show His gen - tle   ways   to   my friends at school today.

Famous Prayers

People just like you have been talking to God in prayer ever since time began. Some prayers are so wonderful that they have become famous. Here are some of those famous prayers. You might like to pray one of these prayers yourself some time.

Father, We Thank Thee

For flowers that bloom about our feet,
    Father, we thank Thee,
For tender grass so fresh and sweet,
    Father, we thank Thee,
For the song of bird and hum of bee,
For all things fair we hear or see,
Father in heaven, we thank Thee.

For blue of stream and blue of sky,
    Father, we thank Thee,
For pleasant shade of branches high,
    Father, we thank Thee,
For fragrant air and cooling breeze,

For beauty of the blooming trees,
Father in heaven, we thank Thee.

For this new morning with its light,
    Father, we thank Thee,
For rest and shelter of the night,
    Father, we thank Thee,
For health and food, for love and friends,
For everything Thy goodness sends,
Father in heaven, we thank Thee.

—RALPH WALDO EMERSON

Good-Night Prayer

Father, unto Thee I pray,
Thou hast guarded me all day;
Safe I am while in Thy sight,
Safely let me sleep tonight.

Bless my friends, the whole world bless;
Help me to learn helpfulness;
Keep me ever in Thy sight;
So to all I say good night.

—HENRY JOHNSTONE

America

Our Fathers' God, to Thee,
Author of liberty,
To Thee we sing.
Long may our land be bright
With freedom's holy light;
Protect us by Thy might,
Great God, our King!

—SAMUEL FRANCIS SMITH

He Prayeth Well,
Who Loveth Well

He prayeth well, who loveth well
Both man and bird and beast.

He prayeth best, who loveth best
All things both great and small;

For the dear God who loveth us,
He made and loveth all.

—SAMUEL TAYLOR COLERIDGE

from *The Rime of the Ancient Mariner*

Jesus,
Tender Shepherd,
Hear Me

Jesus, tender Shepherd, hear me;
    Bless Thy little lamb tonight;
Through the darkness be Thou near me,
    Watch my sleep till morning light.

All this day Thy hand has led me,
    And I thank Thee for Thy care;
Thou has warmed and clothed and fed me;
    Listen to my evening prayer.

—MARY L. DUNCAN

Bedtime Prayer

Now I lay me down to sleep;
I pray Thee, Lord, my soul to keep.
If I should die before I wake,
I pray Thee, Lord, my soul to take.

—AUTHOR UNKNOWN

Doxology

Praise God, from whom all blessings flow;
Praise Him, all creatures here below;
Praise Him above, ye heavenly host:
Praise Father, Son, and Holy Ghost. Amen.

—THOMAS KEN

The Four Freedoms

God, keep this country free:
    Free from tyrants and their whips
    To stamp out truth and seal the lips;
Free for every race and creed,
    Free from fear,
    Free from need;
God, keep this country free.

—LEAH GALE

Jesus, from Thy Throne on High

Jesus, from Thy throne on high,
    Far above the bright blue sky,
Look on me with loving eye;
    Hear me, Holy Jesus.

Be Thou with me every day,
    In my work and in my play,
When I learn and when I pray;
    Hear me , Holy Jesus.

—THOMAS B. POLLOCK

Grace

Be present at our table, Lord;
Be here and everywhere adored.
Thy creatures bless, and grant that we
May feast in paradise with Thee.

—JOHN WESLEY

Prayers for Important Days

$\mathcal{S}$pecial days. Don't you just love them?
Birthdays and Christmas and Easter–they're
the best of all, don't you think? There are
some other special and important days, too. . .
days like Mother's Day and Father's Day or
Thanksgiving with all the food!

Prayer is a wonderful part of important
days. And the prayers in this section of the
book will help you to talk to God on these very
special days. God never takes a holiday–He'll
always be home when you call on Him, even
on important days.

Birthday

Dear God, today is my birthday, and I'm so excited! Thank You, God, for letting me be born. Thank You for making me just as I am. Help me to always live my life just as You want me to. I love You, Father. Amen.

Christmas

Dear Father, thank You for sending Jesus to the earth to save me. It must have hurt You to let Him leave heaven and come down here. I know that means that You love me a lot. And I love You, too, God, more than anything. Thank You for Jesus. Amen.

Easter

O Lord, it's such a wonderful Sunday! It must have been a day just like this when You raised Jesus from the dead. I wish I could have been there to see it. Thank You, God, for bringing Jesus back to life. I know that He lives today and that He is the only One who can save me. Thank You. Amen.

First Day of School

My dear God, I'm really nervous today. It's the first day of school, and I'm a little scared. I'm excited to see all my friends again. Will they still like me as much as they did last year? Will I be able to do the schoolwork in this new grade? Will I have a nice teacher? Please help me to be brave, Father. And please make me feel that You're with me today...all day long. I love You, Lord. In Jesus' name. Amen.

Thanksgiving

Dear Father, this is a special day for us to say thank You for all the beautiful things You do for us. Thank You, God, first of all for Jesus who died to save us from our sins. Thank You for the church where we can meet with other people who believe in You and help each other. Thank You for my family and the love we share. Father, thank You for my friends and teachers at church and at school. And thank You for our food, clothes, and nice place to live. You're so good to us, God, and we love You very much. Help us to remember to thank You every day. Amen.

Mother's Day

Dear Lord, thank You for my mom. She's a great mom, and I love her so much. Help me to show her how much I love her today, God. And please help me to be kind and nice to her every day, not just on Mother's Day. You did a great job when You made my mom, Lord. Thanks! I love You. In the name of Jesus. Amen.

Father's Day

Dear Father, I really love my dad. He takes such good care of me and my family. He works hard, but he also has time for us. He teaches me lots of new things, too, Lord, and I like that. Please bless my dad today, Lord. And help me to show him how much I love him. He's a lot like You, I think. Thanks for giving him to me. In Christ's name. Amen.

People I Want to Pray For

These next pages are for you to write on. You might like to write down the names of people who need your prayers. That will help you remember to pray for them often.

My Family

_____

_____

_____

_____

_____

_____

_____

_____

_____

_____

_____

My Family

_____

_____

_____

_____

_____

_____

_____

_____

_____

_____

_____

_____

My Family

My Family

My Friends

My Friends

My Friends

My Friends

Others

Others

Others

Others

My Prayer Diary

This special part of the book is just for you. Here's how to use it. Each time you pray to God for something special, put down the date and what you prayed. Then carefully listen and watch for God's answer to your prayer. When you know His answer to your prayer, write in the date and how He answered you. This will help you know that God does answer your prayers.

On This Date	I Prayed For	On This Date	God Answered

On This Date	I Prayed For	On This Date	God Answered

On This Date	I Prayed For	On This Date	God Answered

On This Date	I Prayed For	On This Date	God Answered

On This Date	I Prayed For	On This Date	God Answered

On This Date	I Prayed For	On This Date	God Answered

On This Date	I Prayed For	On This Date	God Answered

On This Date	I Prayed For	On This Date	God Answered

On This Date	I Prayed For	On This Date	God Answered

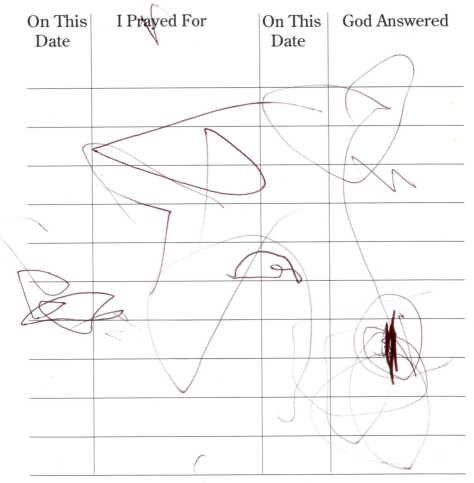

On This Date	I Prayed For	On This Date	God Answered

My Personal Prayers

These next few pages are where you can write your own special prayers. If you need more room, you might like to get a blank notebook to use. Keep on praying!

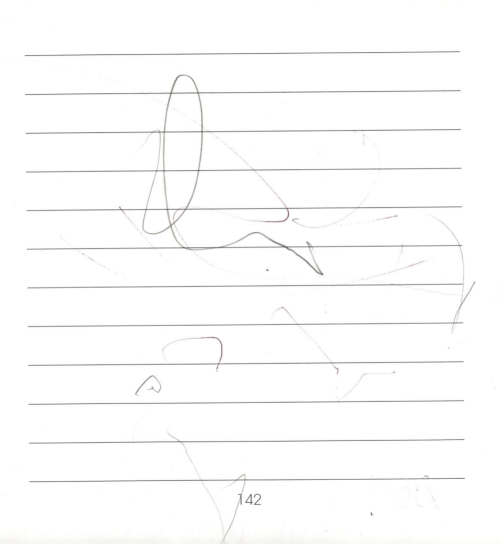

142